21st
Century
Skills Library

COOL CAREERS

PLUMBER

JOSH GREGORY

CHERRY
LAKE
Publishing

Published in the United States of America by
Cherry Lake Publishing, Ann Arbor, Michigan
www.cherrylakepublishing.com

Content Adviser
Nick Lavezzi, Lavezzi Plumbing

Credits
Photos: Cover, pages 1 and 24, ©Monkey Business Images/Dreamstime.com;
page 4, ©iStockphoto.com/kodachrome25; page 6, ©iStockphoto.com/
monkeybusinessimages; page 9, ©iStockphoto.com/Bkhamitsevich; page 10,
©iStockphoto.com/ftwitty; page 12, ©iStockphoto.com/lisafx; page 15, ©iStockphoto.
com/pryzmat; page 16, ©iStockphoto.com/malamus-UK; page 18, ©iStockphoto.com/
sjlocke; page 21, ©James Steidl/Shutterstock, Inc.; page 23, ©iStockphoto.com/
track5; page 27, ©Lisa F. Young/Shutterstock, Inc.; page 28, ©iStockphoto.com/
Andrew_Howe

Library of Congress Cataloging-in-Publication Data
Gregory, Josh.
  Plumber/by Josh Gregory.
     p. cm.—(Cool careers)
  Includes bibliographical references and index.
  ISBN-13: 978-1-60279-984-4 (lib. bdg.)
  ISBN-10: 1-60279-984-9 (lib. bdg.)
  1. Plumbing—Vocational guidance—Juvenile literature. I. Title.
  TH6124.G737 2011
  696'.1023—dc22   2010029538

Cherry Lake Publishing would like to acknowledge
the work of The Partnership for 21st Century Skills.
Please visit *www.21stcenturyskills.org* for more information.

Printed in the United States of America
Corporate Graphics Inc.
January 2011
CLSP08

TABLE OF CONTENTS

CHAPTER ONE
TIME TO CALL A PLUMBER

Steven carefully stepped into the shower and turned the handle for warm water. He had been playing

Plumbers are on the job to keep our sinks, showers, and toilets working.

outside, which had made him very muddy. He picked up the bar of soap and began to wash away the mud. As he scrubbed between his fingers, he noticed something. The water wasn't going down the drain!

Steven quickly turned off the water. "Dad! Something is wrong with the shower!" he called down the hall.

Steven's dad hurried in to see what the problem was. He looked down into the bottom of the shower.

"It looks like we've got a clog," he said. "It will take a long time for this water to drain."

"What will we do?" asked Steven. "We need a working shower to stay clean."

"I think we need to call a plumber," Steven's dad replied. "He'll be able to fix the problem."

■ ■ ■

Plumbers install and help maintain the systems of pipes we use every day. These pipes are known as plumbing systems. Some of these plumbing systems carry water to our homes and businesses. Sinks, bathtubs, and dishwashers are all part of plumbing systems. Other systems help carry waste from toilets or garbage disposals to treatment centers. We also use plumbing systems to bring natural gas into our homes. This gas provides power to stoves, heaters, and other appliances. Plumbers are in charge of creating these systems and making sure that they continue to work correctly.

People like Steven's dad call a plumber to schedule a **house call**. Many plumbers make house calls to help people with clogs, leaks, and other problems in their home plumbing systems. Plumbers know how pipes are connected. They know which pipes carry which things. They also have special tools that help them work on the pipes.

Sometimes plumbers help install new appliances. Dishwashers, water heaters, and many other appliances are all connected to plumbing systems. Plumbers make sure these

Plumbers make house calls to fix problems in home plumbing systems.

appliances are connected the right way. This keeps them from leaking water or damaging the pipes.

Plumbers don't only make house calls. They also plan and install plumbing systems in new buildings or additions to old buildings. They decide where the pipes will go and make sure they are connected the right way. They also connect these pipes to the bigger plumbing systems that run through a town or city. Plumbing systems in places such as restaurants or factories are often more complicated than the systems in a house.

Once the pipes are in place and the building is close to being finished, plumbers install fixtures. Fixtures are what we use to control the plumbing system. They include faucets, showerheads, and toilets. They allow us to fill the sink with water or make the water warm in the shower. Without these fixtures, plumbing systems would not be as useful.

Before anyone starts using a new plumbing system, plumbers need to be sure everything works correctly. They use **pressure gauges** to make sure the water or gas flows at the proper rate. Too much pressure can cause a pipe to explode. Too little pressure can also cause problems. Water might only trickle from a faucet, or a toilet might not flush. After plumbers have checked everything one last time, the plumbing system is ready to go.

Not all plumbing systems are in buildings. Plumbers also install and maintain the larger systems of pipes that run throughout cities and towns. Some of these plumbers work for local governments. They work on city-owned plumbing systems, such as the ones that supply the city's water. Others work for **utility** companies, such as gas providers.

LEARNING & INNOVATION SKILLS

Plumbing systems have been around for a very long time. Some of the earliest indoor bathrooms are about 5,000 years old! These bathrooms were not like the ones we use today. They were little more than holes in the floor that led to pipes that drained out of the building. It wasn't until the late 19th century that indoor plumbing systems similar to those we use today were created. Since then, plumbing systems have gotten better and better. Plumbers continue to make improvements. Can you think of any ways our modern plumbing could be improved?

Plumbers also work at treatment plants. In many places, water that goes down a drain, toilet, or garbage disposal ends up at a **sewage treatment plant**. That is where the water is cleaned before it goes to lakes, rivers, or other natural bodies of water. **Water treatment plants** collect water from wells, lakes, or other sources. Workers use filters

Sewage treatment plants hold large amounts of wastewater.

and chemicals to make the water safe for people to use. Then the water is pumped into large storage tanks. Plumbers help to design these systems and make sure that they always work properly. Without plumbers, people could get sick from **pollution** in the water.

CHAPTER TWO

WHAT PLUMBERS DO

Every day brings new challenges for a plumber. There are many things to keep in mind when installing pipes

Plumbers must carefully review building plans before they start their work.

in a new building. Plumbers begin jobs by planning out the building's plumbing system. They meet with the supervisors of the construction project to discuss the best way to install the plumbing system. They look at **blueprints** to see what the building will look like when it is done. They make sure the pipes won't get in the way of other parts of the building, such as electrical wires.

The plumbers plan the job so they don't use more pipes than they have to. They don't want the system to waste water. They do this by using their knowledge of plumbing systems and **building codes**. Planning this way helps builders save money. It also saves resources, which is good for the environment.

Once the building team has finalized the plans, plumbers can get to work installing pipes. They use many different tools. For some jobs, plumbers must make holes in the ceiling, floor, or walls. Different kinds of saws help them cut holes through the parts of the building where pipes need to go. Careful measurements are very important. Plumbers do not want to cut big holes in walls when they only need room for a small pipe. They also don't want pipes that are too short or too long to fit in a space. They use pipe cutters to make pipes that are the right size for the job. Pipes can also be bent to fit where they need to go.

Different types of pipe are used for different jobs. The pipes in people's homes are usually made of plastic, steel, or copper. Pipes used in a sewer system need to hold the water from all nearby buildings. They are bigger than the pipes used inside houses. They are usually made of a heavy material called cast iron.

Pipes are connected with **fittings**. Fittings look like very short pieces of pipe. They are just a little bit wider than the pipes they connect. The ends of the connecting pipes slide inside the fitting. Some fittings connect two pipes. Others can connect three or four pipes. Some fittings are curved

Pipes and fittings must be tightly connected.

or angled. This helps plumbers install pipes around corners or connect pipes that go in different directions.

Once the pipes are in the fittings, plumbers need to make sure they won't move. For plastic pipes, they use special glue to hold the pipes and the fittings together. Metal pipes are usually **soldered** to their fittings. This means the plumber uses a torch to melt thin pieces of metal onto the pipes and fittings. When the melted metal cools, it becomes hard. This keeps the pipe and the fitting stuck together.

LIFE & CAREER SKILLS

Nick Lavezzi always knew that he wanted to be a plumber. Today, he and his brother run the plumbing business their father started. Even though he loves his job, not every part of it is fun. "A lot of nasty things come with this job," he says. "Opening up clogged pipes can get dirty and stinky, and sometimes you have to squeeze into a crawl space where there isn't much room to move." All the nasty parts are worth it in the end, though. "I always like getting compliments from happy customers," Lavezzi says. "It's satisfying to see that everything looks nice and works."

Some plumbers specialize in working with certain kinds of pipe systems. Pipelayers are experts who work with underground pipe systems like sewers. They use heavy construction equipment to dig trenches in the ground. They lay pipes in the trenches and then fill in the holes.

Pipefitters don't work with regular water plumbing systems. Instead, they install special pipe systems for electricity, heating systems, and other uses. They often work in factories where special pipe systems are needed to make products.

Sprinkler fitters install sprinkler systems. These sprinkler systems detect fires and spray water to help put them out.

21ST CENTURY CONTENT

Sprinkler systems are often found in schools, offices, and stores. Today, more and more people are choosing to install these helpful systems in their homes. Sprinklers can help put out fires before they spread to other rooms or cause serious damage. These systems can easily be installed in new and existing homes. As demand for sprinklers grows, more sprinkler fitters will be needed to help keep homes safe from fires.

Pipelayers often work on large, underground plumbing systems.

No matter what kinds of jobs they do, all people who want to become plumbers need to spend time learning before they can go to work.

CHAPTER THREE
BECOMING A PLUMBER

E ven though different plumbers do different things, there are certain skills every plumber needs.

Working in tight spaces is often part of a plumber's day.

Every plumber needs to be able to follow directions. Sometimes this means they have to pay close attention to the instructions their supervisors give them. Other times, it means they need to know how to read and follow blueprints and other designs. It takes special training to be able to understand the drawings and measurements on these designs.

Plumbers also need to be physically fit. Many plumbers have to lift and carry large pipes and heavy tools. They sometimes work long hours and don't have much time for breaks. Some jobs require plumbers to stand in uncomfortable positions. They might need to squeeze into tight spaces or crouch down. They need to be strong and energetic to succeed.

Efficiency is also important to plumbers. They often have busy schedules and can't afford to waste time. In order to get more work done each day, they need to plan carefully. They must make sure to bring the right tools and supplies to each job.

Plumbing systems can be found almost anywhere. This means plumbers work in many different places. Some plumbers work mostly in buildings that are still under construction. Other plumbers work more often in homes, offices, and factories that have already been built.

Pipelayers and other experts who work on underground pipe systems usually work outdoors. Sometimes they have to work in bad weather. When underground pipes burst due to freezing, plumbers have to bundle up and head out into the cold to fix the problem.

Construction sites can be loud, dangerous places. Plumbers must be careful to avoid getting hurt on the job. Hot pipes or soldering torches can burn careless plumbers. Plumbers might wear gloves to protect their hands. They also need to be careful when standing on tall ladders or using sharp tools.

Some plumbers specialize in working on new construction.

Students who are planning to become plumbers should take classes in a variety of topics. Courses in English and Spanish or another foreign language help build communication skills. These skills can help plumbers work with clients, supervisors, and fellow plumbers. It is especially useful for plumbers who hope to run their own businesses.

Science courses such as physics and chemistry are also important. They help plumbers understand how and why plumbing systems work. This can help them get better at designing and planning systems on their own. It can also help them to figure out the causes of certain plumbing problems.

You do not need a college degree to become a plumber. That doesn't mean plumbers don't have to spend time learning the job, though. Some plumbers choose to attend technical schools or community colleges. Others join plumbing unions, which offer training programs. Either way, these future plumbers will work **apprenticeships** and take classes. These classes help them learn basic skills about blueprints, safety, and different kinds of plumbing systems. Apprentices also take classes in math, chemistry, and physics.

Apprenticeships usually last 4 or 5 years. Apprentices work beside more experienced plumbers. They get valuable on-the-job experience. Apprentices learn to do more difficult jobs as they gain experience and skills. Apprentices are usually paid about half as much as fully trained plumbers.

A future plumber must be at least 18 years old to begin an apprenticeship. Most apprenticeships require a high school diploma.

LIFE & CAREER SKILLS

Many plumbers living in North America belong to the United Association of Journeymen and Apprentices of the Plumbing and Pipe Fitting Industry of the United States and Canada (UA). It was started in 1889. The union has about 326,000 members throughout the United States and Canada. Local union offices offer training programs and help members find work in the area. There are more than 300 local UA offices in North America. For more information, visit www.ua.org

A plumber's education does not end after the apprenticeship is over. According to plumber Nick Lavezzi, "You learn a lot with an apprenticeship, but a lot of what you know comes from learning on the job. You might make mistakes at first, but it becomes natural after a while. It gets to be so you don't even have to think about it, you just always know what to do."

Apprenticeships help plumbers learn the skills they will need throughout their careers.

Most states or cities require plumbers to become licensed before they can work. This usually means they need to take a test to prove that they have the knowledge and skills to be a good plumber. They might also need a certain amount of experience as an apprentice. Many experienced plumbers continue to take classes and learn about new types of plumbing systems and the latest tools. This helps them stay up-to-date with modern technology.

LIFE & CAREER SKILLS

Plumbers in many states must take some classes to renew their plumbing licenses. Each state has its own rules. Plumbers in Washington must take 8 hours of classes every year. Plumbers in New Jersey only need 5 hours of classes every 2 years. All plumbers need to know their state's licensing rules. If they can't renew their licenses, they can't work!

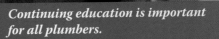
Continuing education is important for all plumbers.

CHAPTER FOUR
LOOKING INTO THE FUTURE

The future looks bright for plumbers. In 2008, there were about 555,900 people working as plumbers. That number is expected to increase 16 percent by 2018.

Plumbers will be in demand in the future.

Plumbers are paid well for their hard work. Most of them earn between $16.63 and $29.66 an hour. Some of the most experienced plumbers make more than $37.93 an hour. The lowest-paid plumbers make less than $13.22 an hour.

About a third of all plumbers belong to unions. Unions help plumbers get apprenticeships and find jobs. They also help make sure plumbers are paid fairly and receive good benefits, such as health insurance.

New technology will be an important part of plumbers' jobs in the future. Some people live in very dry places, such as Arizona or New Mexico. These areas do not get much rain. There are not many bodies of water close by. People living there need to protect and conserve their water supplies. Plumbers will use new technology to help these people save water. New types of appliances can save water in homes. Special **irrigation** systems help farmers water their crops without wasting.

More and more builders and homeowners are becoming interested in creating environmentally friendly buildings. This is known as the "green" movement. Saving water is an important part of the green movement. Plumbers will need to learn about new plumbing technology. They can take classes to become certified green plumbers. The classes teach plumbers about ways to recycle water and prevent systems from wasting clean water. This might include designing systems to collect and clean rainwater. Plumbers also learn how to design plumbing systems that use less energy.

21ST CENTURY CONTENT

The average person uses 80 to 100 gallons (303 to 379 liters) of water each day. We need to work on decreasing our water usage. Plumbers can help by designing more efficient plumbing systems and installing better equipment. There are also things you can do at home to help. Be careful not to run faucets longer than necessary. Try not to run the faucet while you brush your teeth or wash dishes. Ask your parents to check for leaks. Even small leaks can add up to a lot of wasted water. Follow these tips and you can save hundreds of gallons of water!

Solar energy is another important part of the green movement. Plumbers can learn to install solar-powered water-heating systems. They can also learn how to install this new technology into older systems. Learning these skills will help them find work as people become more interested in protecting the environment.

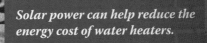

Solar power can help reduce the energy cost of water heaters.

Our lives would be very different without the work of plumbers. Showers, sinks, and many other things we use daily are in our homes because of plumbers. One day you too could have a job keeping our plumbing systems working. Do you have what it takes?

Do you think you would enjoy a plumbing career?

SOME WELL-KNOWN PLUMBERS

Sir John Harington (1561–1612) was the inventor of the flush toilet. He came up with the idea in the late 16th century. He installed it in a palace belonging to his godmother, Queen Elizabeth I. Harington was also a successful translator and writer.

George Meany (1894–1980) was a plumber who became an important labor leader in the early 20th century. He is best known for helping to combine two unions, the American Federation of Labor (AFL) and the Congress of Industrial Organizations (CIO). These groups united into one powerful union, the AFL-CIO. Meany received the Presidential Medal of Freedom in 1963.

P. J. Quinlan was the cofounder and first general president of the United Association of Journeymen and Apprentices of the Plumbing and Pipe Fitting Industry of the United States and Canada (UA). He started the union in 1889 by writing a letter to a fellow plumber named Richard A. O'Brien. The UA has since become an important part of the plumbing industry in North America.

GLOSSARY

apprenticeships (uh-PREN-tiss-shipss) on-the-job training during which people learn a trade by working with experienced professionals

blueprints (BLOO-printss) plans for building something

building codes (BIL-ding KOHDZ) rules about how a building has to be built

efficiency (uh-FISH-uhn-see) the ability to do something without wasting time, money, or materials

fittings (FIT-ingz) pieces that are used to connect pipes to each other

house call (HOUSS KAWL) a visit by a worker to someone's home to fix a problem or provide a service

irrigation (ihr-uh-GAY-shuhn) the process of watering farmland through artificial means such as sprinklers or pipe systems

pollution (puh-LOO-shuhn) harmful waste

pressure gauges (PRESH-ur GAYJ-ihz) tools that show how much force water or gas is putting on a plumbing system

sewage treatment plant (SOO-ij TREET-muhnt PLANT) a place where wastewater is cleaned before being sent back into the water system

soldered (SOD-urd) joined together with melted metal

utility (yoo-TIL-uh-tee) a service such as water or electricity

water treatment plants (WAW-tur TREET-muhnt PLANTSS) places where water is cleaned before being sent to homes or businesses

FOR MORE INFORMATION

BOOKS

Barnhill, Kelly Regan. *Sewers and the Rats That Love Them: The Disgusting Story Behind Where It All Goes*. Mankato, MN: Capstone Press, 2009.

Raum, Elizabeth. *The Story Behind Toilets*. Chicago: Heinemann Library, 2009.

WEB SITES

Bureau of Labor Statistics: Plumbers, Pipelayers, Pipefitters, and Steamfitters
www.bls.gov/oco/ocos211.htm
Interested in plumbing careers? Find out more at this site.

EPA: Simple Ways to Save Water
www.epa.gov/watersense/kids/simpleways.html
Learn about ways you can save water at home.

United Association—Union of Plumbers, Fitters, Welders, and HVAC Service Techs
www.ua.org
Learn more about training and apprenticeships from this major North American plumbers' union.

INDEX

ABOUT THE AUTHOR

Josh Gregory writes and edits books for kids. He lives in Chicago, Illinois. Luckily, he has never had any plumbing problems in his home.